How to do Search Engine Optimization (SEO) and Monetization

of YouTube Videos

Content

8. How to SEO YouTube Video

9. Conclusion.

Prologue

There are many videos on YouTube which has more than 50 million views. The average income from 1 million views is $1000, so with 50 million views the income of the person who made the video is $50000 from Google AdSense; but if the video contained some information about a product and he had 10000 visits to his website and a single person paid $10 on average then the income of that person from the video is $100000. AdSense pays you peanuts ($1000) in comparison to money you might have made from the video. Be creative, have a concept or a product behind the video. If your video becomes viral then the cash bells of your website start ringing.

The Digital Version of Book is available at:

http://www.amazon.com/gp/product/B01D1UW0XK

Chapter One: How to create a YouTube Video

The simplest way to make video is to record it through your smartphone and then upload it on YouTube, but that video will look very crude –there will be no aesthetics in it. Another option is to download the software EM PowerPoint to video convertor and then prepare a slideshow of 10-15 slides and convert it into MPEG4 file. You can also download some good background music and attach it during the conversion process so that the video has background music in it.

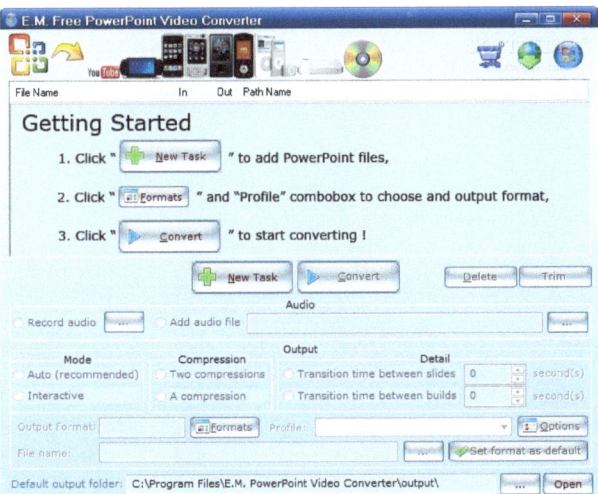

There are host of video creator and free music services on web, with the help of which you can create a video.

But I outline the simplest steps to create a video:

- Make a PowerPoint presentation
- In file option select Save and Send
- Choose the Video Option
- In Video option select timing as 8 seconds
- Then choose the Internet and HD option in the video
- Allow the PPT to be converted into .wmv format
- Upload it on YouTube

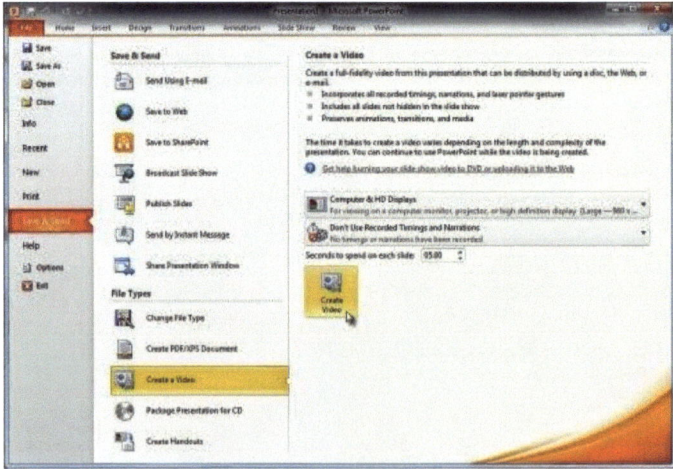

When your video is processed on YouTube, publish it, check the video after playing it. Like the video and put a good comment in the comment field.

Chapter Two: Adding Sound to YouTube Video

When you have uploaded the video on YouTube then you can have a separate sound file and attach the sound file to the video on YouTube at a later stage. If you have prepared video through smartphone then the sound is already in it.

If you use web service to prepare a video then there are websites which offer free sound clips. You can download free sound clips from these sites and embed it in the video.

If you are using EM PowerPoint to video convertor then you can embed the sound file while conversion from PPT to MPEG4 file is taking place.

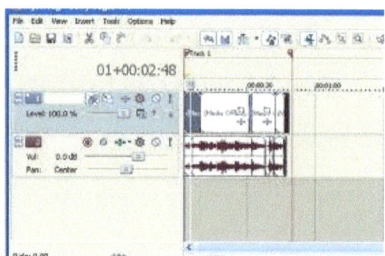

Chapter Three: Monetization of YouTube Video

Now I will teach you —how to monetize your YouTube videos. The process is very simple. Make two generic videos with no promotional stuff and upload it on YouTube. Once two videos are uploaded on YouTube, wait for two days and garner views, likes and comments to your videos with the help of like4like.org.

Once both videos have 25 likes and 25 comments –the videos cross the brink of becoming viral and they would feature prominently in YouTube searches. Then follow the simple process mentioned below for monetization:

- Log in to your YouTube account
- Search for AdSense for YouTube in Google
- In the page displayed click on the link which states –I do not have AdSense account
- Then fill the AdSense form with your name, address and mobile number
- Then link your YouTube account to AdSense

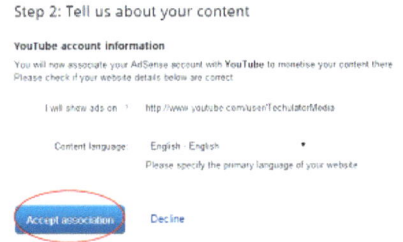

- Accept the YouTube terms and conditions for monetization
- Select the previously loaded two videos for monetization
- Also select the inlay video card for monetization besides the three format for monetization
- Log back and your YouTube and AdSense accounts are linked
- Keep monetizing your further videos by selecting the monetization tab, while publishing the video.

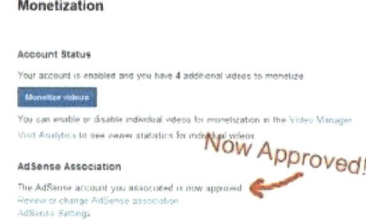

There are lot of tutorials available on YouTube –how to monetize your videos.

Please check:

https://www.youtube.com/watch?v=5zoAWgabKL8

Chapter Four: Importance of SEO of YouTube Video

Suppose you search for "Hanuman Chalisa" in Google and your video comes at the first three results of Google search, then can you imagine how many views your video will get and how much revenue your video will earn? In simple arithmetic calculation –one view to your video earns you $0.001. So if your video has one million views then earning from one video would be close to $1000.

There are two types of search through which a person can search your video. The first search is the Google Search –and for given keywords, if your video has prominent ranking –then there would be lot of views to your video.

The second way through which someone can reach your video is through the internal search in YouTube.

The third way someone can view your video is through the featured video –when your video is featured along with other videos –which run on YouTube.

But there are three categories of videos:

- One which gets less than 10K views
- One which gets 10k -1 million views

- One which gets above 1 million views

The videos which get above 1 million views are viral videos –they have the keywords and content which catches the eye of viewer. So to increase the views – target on keywords and content.

The videos which go viral are mostly from films and songs. The song "Why this Kolaveri Di" got 40 million views within one month mostly due to word-of-mouth; though the film flopped.

What you can do is to download the song of movie from a MP3 site, and then make a collage with stills from the movie with music playing in background. The Juke Box is also a major hit at YouTube –with collection of good songs and stills from movie playing in background. The "Arijit Singh Hit Songs" and "Atif Aslam Hit Story" had more than 33 million views.

The topics on which you should make video to go viral are:

- Films
- Bhajans
- Songs
- Religion
- Spirituality
- Fail Collection
- Accidents
- Adventure
- Jokes
- Kids and Toys
- Top 10

- Top 5
- How to do
- Education
- Cooking
- Stunts
- Parody
- Comedy
- Games

The number of subscribers also plays an important role in making the video viral. Suppose if you have 10000 subscribers and 1000 of them views your video when it is published –then immediately the ranking of your video increases.

Chapter Five: Benefits from YouTube Video

There are multiple benefits of a YouTube video. These benefits are outlined below:

- It helps your product to get recognized
- It helps your product to go viral
- You will have constant flow of traffic due to YouTube videos

- You will have constant customers due to YouTube videos
- You will have an additional source of revenue
- You can get your viewpoint heard
- You can create a fan base
- You can get backers for your idea

The Digital Version of Book is available at:
http://www.amazon.com/gp/product/B01D1UW0XK

Chapter Six: Making YouTube Video Viral in Social Media

There are multiple ways through which you can make your video viral in social media. These methods are outlined below:

- You can organize a contest in video and ask your followers to participate
- You can synchronize the retweets of large number of people about your video
- You can reddit it to go viral
- You can post the link of your video in other viral videos
- You can share your video in Facebook groups
- You can share your video in LinkedIn groups
- You can share your video in Google Plus circles to make it viral
- You can exchange your videos in sites like likesplanet, like4like, followlike etc for views for views
- You can follow the steps given in book:
  How to do Viral Marketing – The steps in making Business or Website Viral:

http://www.amazon.com/gp/product/B01BRCMA7K

- You can run campaigns at traffic exchanges to make it viral.

Chapter Seven: How to SEO YouTube Video

There are multiple factors on which the search engine ranking and internal YouTube ranking of a video depends. These are:

- Number of views
- Number of likes and dislikes

- Number of comments

- Keywords in title
- Keywords in description of video
- Keywords in the tag of video
- Number of subscribers of channel
- External links to the video
- Popularity of the video
- Competition in the niche

Now I will elucidate it with the help of an example. Suppose you have to make a video on "Seven Wonders of Lord Jagannath Temple in Puri, Orissa", then how you will go about it.

Ideally:

- You should name the title: "Seven (7) wonders of Lord Jagannath Temple –Puri, Orissa, India"
- You should make description as: "This video explains seven magnificent wonders of Lord Jagannath Temple –Puri, Orissa, India. Please like the video and subscribe to my channel."
- The tags should go as:
    1. Seven wonders of Lord Jagannath Temple
    2. Puri, Orissa, India
    3. Sun Temple
    4. Lord Vishnu Temple
    5. 7 Wonders
    6. Magnificent Puri Temple
    7. Puri Temple Orissa
    8. Lord Vishnu Magnificent
    9. Devotee of Lord Vishnu
    10. Lord Vishnu Mantra
    11. Lord Vishnu Miracle

These tags should generate a large number of searches with the permutation and combination of keywords.

Next you go to the site like4like.org and attach the link of video in the sections "YouTube Likes", "YouTube comment".

Keep earning points in like4like.org until you get 100 likes and 100 comments. After getting 100 likes and 100 comments, your video will start showing high up in the internal and external search results.

Then go to site followlike.net and get another 100 like and 100 comments for your video. Now this video is fully optimized.

After that put link of this video in 100 videos on related topics or on topics of religion and spirituality. Thus 100 links to your video is generated. Next go to fiverr.com or seoclerk.com and for $5-$10 order scrapebox blast for the video. There would thousands of external links pointing towards the video.

SCRAPE BOX
blست

Then using traffup.net, get your video re-tweeted to as many people you possibly could. After that put your video as a link in reddit.com and generate swarms of views to your video. Start sharing your video in at least 40 Facebook groups and 40 LinkedIn groups. This will generate views as well as backlinks. Once you are done with the steps mentioned, your video is fully optimized for search results and your video will get natural flow of traffic. 5% of dislikes in comparison to likes also help the video to get higher search rankings.

Chapter 8: Conclusion

Lastly I would like to say that make videos on popular topics so that you can have maximum number of views. You can get hint by analyzing videos which have more than 10 million views.

This is the latest trend and many people are rushing to join this bandwagon. Off late I got two warnings from YouTube that the content of my video is inappropriate and I will have one strike in my account for next six months.

Google must be doing this to control spam on YouTube, and when I go to like4like.org to increase my twitter followers then I see mad rush of You Tubers who are trying to increase their likes and subscribers.

To be honest with you I make only $60 per month from YouTube for my 30 Videos. But if I had 3000 videos, I would be making $6000 per month from YouTube. But guys like PewDiePie, Swosh and Jenna Marbles are making $1 Million to $5 Million per Year from YouTube.

People who join this mad rush are skeptical about creating videos. But creating Video is not a tough task. You can make a presentation in Power Point and can convert it into video through EM Power Point to Video convertor. You can also record a video through your Smartphone and upload it on YouTube.

If you earn significantly through YouTube, you can purchase a camcorder and learn video editing skills to make great videos. You can use these skills to create great Udemy courses too.

But there are some restrictions from Google to prevent the misuse of YouTube. People often put their affiliate links in description tag of their videos. To prevent suspension of your account, you should never promote your clickbank links through YouTube. (Google may clamp hard on you).

(When I analyzed the number of clicks which I received through video description then I found out that there were barely 7-8 clicks in a month. So never leave a link in the description tag of your video. The best option would be to leave a link in final segment of your video and that should not be clickable.)

The Digital Version of Book is available at:

http://www.amazon.com/gp/product/B01D1UW0XK

End of Book